Xtreme Fishing

FLY FISHING

BY S.L. HAMILTON

A&D Xtreme
An imprint of Abdo Publishing | www.abdopublishing.com

Visit us at
www.abdopublishing.com

Published by Abdo Publishing Company, a division of ABDO, PO Box 398166, Minneapolis, Minnesota 55439. Copyright ©2015 by Abdo Consulting Group, Inc. International copyrights reserved in all countries. No part of this book may be reproduced in any form without written permission from the publisher. A&D Xtreme™ is a trademark and logo of Abdo Publishing Company.

Printed in the United States of America, North Mankato, Minnesota.
092014
012015

Editor: John Hamilton
Graphic Design: Sue Hamilton
Cover Design: Sue Hamilton
Cover Photo: AlaskaStock
Interior Photos: Alamy-pgs 20-21, 24-25 & 26-27; AlaskaStock-pg 19; AP-pgs 6-7; Glow Images-pgs 12, 13 & 28; iStock-pgs 1, 2-3, 8-9, 10-11, 18, 22-23, 26 (lure graphic) & 32; James Smedley-pgs 14-15 & 16-17, Minden Pictures-pgs 30-31; RavenFire Media-pg 26 (inset).

Websites
To learn more about Fishing, visit booklinks.abdopublishing.com. These links are routinely monitored and updated to provide the most current information available.

Library of Congress Control Number: 2014944875

Cataloging-in-Publication Data

Hamilton, S.L.
 Fly fishing / S.L. Hamilton.
  p. cm. -- (Xtreme fishing)
ISBN 978-1-62403-680-4 (lib. bdg.)
Includes index.
1. Fly fishing--Juvenile literature.   I. Title.
799.12/4--dc23

2014944875

Contents

Fly Fishing

Fly fishing requires anglers to use a special rod and reel with a weighted fishing line. Artificial "flies" are nearly weightless lures. They are tied to the heavy fly line.

Fly fishing takes a lot of practice. Skilled anglers know how to cast their lines so the flies land in a spot where fish are waiting to strike. People fly fish in freshwater lakes and streams, as well as saltwater shorelines. It is part art, part skill, and part adventure.

XTREME QUOTE –
"*There is no greater fan of fly fishing than the worm.*"

–Patrick McManus, outdoorsman and author

Rods & Reels

Fly fishing reels are loaded with heavy line. This allows anglers to cast the nearly weightless lures out in front of the fish.

XTREME FACT – In general, a 9-foot (2.7-m) -long, 5-weight rod is a good trout rod. For bigger saltwater fish, such as tarpon, a 9-foot (2.7 m) -long, 12-weight rod is needed.

Fly fishing rods differ by length, shape, and weight. Rods are numbered by the weight of the line it should be paired with. For example, a 3-weight rod uses a lighter line than a 12-weight rod. Anglers pick rods based on where they are fishing (creek, river, lake, or sea) and how heavy a fish they are trying to catch.

Flies

Fly fishermen use one of three different types of lures: dry flies, wet flies (nymphs), and streamers.

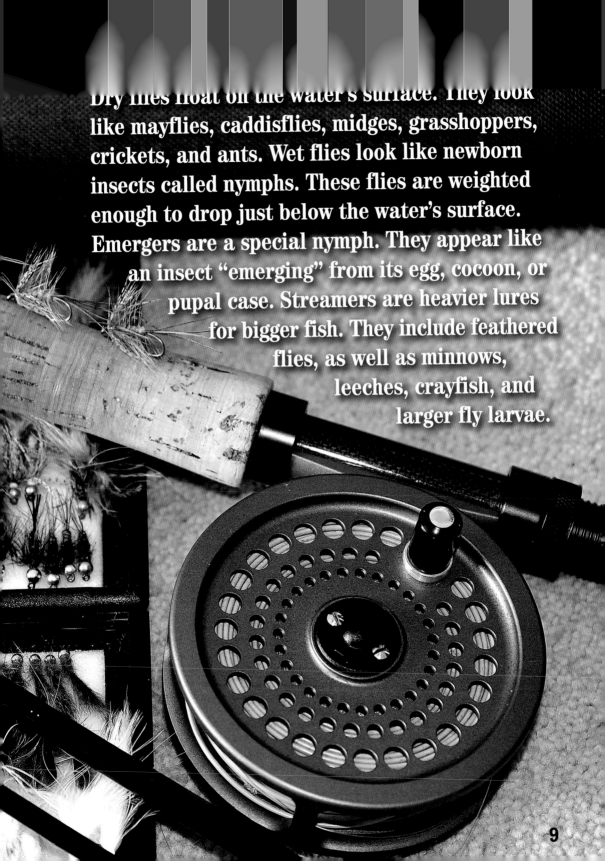

Dry flies float on the water's surface. They look like mayflies, caddisflies, midges, grasshoppers, crickets, and ants. Wet flies look like newborn insects called nymphs. These flies are weighted enough to drop just below the water's surface. Emergers are a special nymph. They appear like an insect "emerging" from its egg, cocoon, or pupal case. Streamers are heavier lures for bigger fish. They include feathered flies, as well as minnows, leeches, crayfish, and larger fly larvae.

Waders & Boots

To get close to the fish, fly fishermen often stand in water. Two of the most important pieces of equipment are waders and a good pair of boots. Waders are hip, waist, or chest high. They are often made of Gore-Tex fabric, which keeps the angler dry, but not too sweaty. Some waders come with a floatation safety belt. Additionally, studded rubber wading boots give good traction, as well as protect the feet from sharp objects.

XTREME FACT– A pair of polarized sunglasses helps anglers see pockets of fish in the water.

Float Tubes & Boats

Float tubes allow anglers to quietly move closer to the fish. The tubes weigh only 4 to 10 pounds (2 to 5 kg) and are often carried in backpacks to remote lakes. Anglers may wear flippers to help propel their float tubes.

Flipper

XTREME FACT – Float tubes were developed when fly fishermen first used inner tubes to float and fish from.

Pontoon boats used by fly fishermen are bigger, sturdier, and much heavier than float tubes. They weigh about 65 pounds (29 kg). Pontoons sometimes have motors, but are often propelled with oars. Poke boats are a combination of a float tube and a pontoon boat. These stable watercraft are propelled by oars. They are lightweight, about 14 pounds (6 kg).

Trout

Trout are a favorite catch of many fly fishermen. Brook, brown, and rainbow trout feed on small insects. Fly fishermen mimic these insects with their lures. Anglers walk, wade, or float quietly and slowly into clear, freshwater streams and lakes. Trout sense vibrations around them, and they can see movement. Fly fishermen stay behind the trout, then drop a dry fly, nymph, or streamer in front of their prey. It takes skill and style to drop a fly in a realistic enough manner to make a trout bite. It is challenging and exciting to catch one's limit of delicious trout.

XTREME FACT– Trout may weigh from 1 to 8 pounds (.5 - 3.6 kg). A group of rainbow trout is called a hover.

Steelhead

Steelhead are a species of rainbow trout. These popular sport fish typically weigh about 8 pounds (3.6 kg), but may reach up to 50 pounds (23 kg). Fly fishermen use the dead drift technique to catch steelhead. The angler casts a nymph or wet fly upstream and allows it to float with the current of the stream. Steelhead usually wait for their meals to float to them.

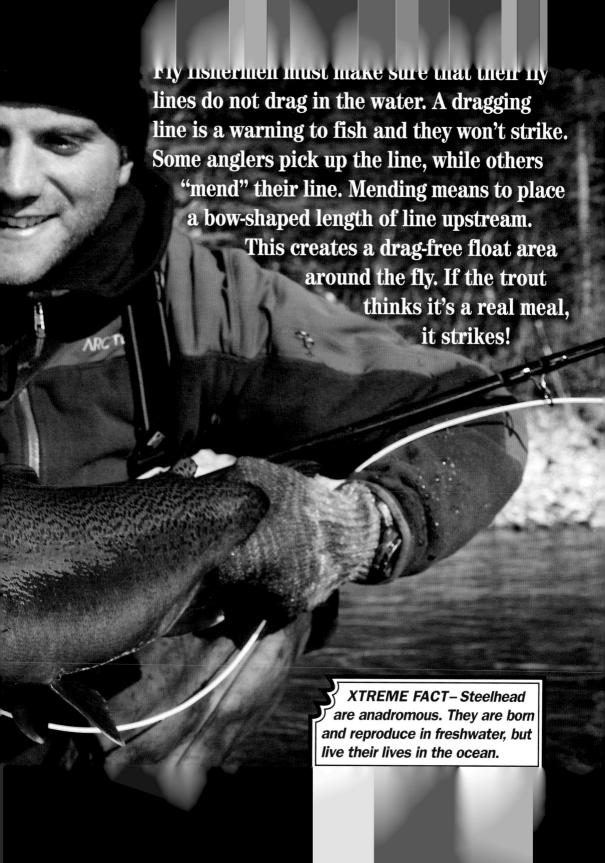

Fly fishermen must make sure that their fly lines do not drag in the water. A dragging line is a warning to fish and they won't strike. Some anglers pick up the line, while others "mend" their line. Mending means to place a bow-shaped length of line upstream. This creates a drag-free float area around the fly. If the trout thinks it's a real meal, it strikes!

XTREME FACT – Steelhead are anadromous. They are born and reproduce in freshwater, but live their lives in the ocean.

Salmon

When hooked, salmon leap, twist, thrash and jump with power and force. Heavier 8-weight rods and line are needed to catch these big fish. Coho or silver salmon weigh between 5 and 10 pounds (2 to 5 kg). Chinook are even bigger, reaching up to 43 pounds (20 kg).

Silver Salmon

Fly fishermen usually use streamers to catch salmon. Sometimes the color of the fly makes a big difference. Some anglers say that green, orange, and yellow flies attract the fish's attention in the spring, while red-colored flies work best in the fall. But what works one day, may not work the next.

Chinook Salmon

Tarpon

Tarpon, or silvers, are saltwater fish known for their huge leaps, somersaults, and fast runs. They may be in open water or may move near the shore to feed and rest. They are often seen "busting" out of the water. This is when their backs and heads appear on the surface. These huge fish average 40 to 100 pounds (18 to 45 kg), but may reach sizes over 200 pounds (91 kg). Fly fishermen need a sturdy 12-weight fishing rod to catch tarpon.

XTREME FACT – Tarpon are not good eating, but are very exciting to catch. Most people practice "catch and release" with tarpon.

To get a tarpon to bite, fishermen cast a fly so it lands in front of the fish. They then move the fly away from the fish. (Real flies would never move toward a tarpon.) If the fly line or its shadow crosses the fish, it will spook. But if it bites, chasing and catching tarpon is excitement on a hook.

Bonefish

Bonefish are found in the shallow, tropical waters of the Atlantic and Pacific Oceans, and the Caribbean Sea. Bonefish average 2 to 14 pounds (1 to 6 kg). An 8-weight rod is needed.

Bonefish are easy to see swimming in the clear water near shorelines. Fly fishermen go "sight fishing." An angler targets a specific bonefish in the water, dropping what looks like a tasty fly right in front of it. Bonefish are exciting catches. They move with speed and power away from the angler when hooked.

XTREME FACT – Bonefish are so called because of their many small bones. They are also known as gray ghosts and flats phantoms.

Permit

Fly fishermen search for permits near shore in saltwater flats. Their white, reflective skin makes them nearly invisible. A 15- to 20-pound (7- to 9-kg) permit may surface enough to show its dorsal fin or the tip of its tail above the waterline.

XTREME FACT – Fly fishermen usually wade in the water to catch permit.

To keep the big-eyed permit from spooking, a fly fisherman casts into the wind at a great distance. The angler drops the fly 15 to 20 feet (5 to 6 m) in front of the fish, then moves the lure enough to get the permit's attention. When it bites, the angler knows he's done everything right to catch this wily, hard-fighting fish.

Striped Bass

Stripers are saltwater fish sought for their size, taste, and battling ability. They grow up to 30 pounds (14 kg), so a strong 10- to 12-weight rod is needed. Fly fishermen seek stripers near shorelines at dusk and dawn.

XTREME FACT–To keep from scaring away fish at greater depths, an angler will attach a leader and tippet to the fly line. Underwater, the leader and tippet are nearly invisible. The fly drops and the fish bites!

FLY LINE

LEADER   TIPPET

Dangers

Fly fishing can be dangerous. Many anglers have been impaled by hooks when casting. Fly fishermen wear hats to protect their heads from hooks, as well as from the sun. Anglers need to get inside when bad weather approaches. Some fly fishing poles act as lightning rods. Anglers often seek great fishing spots in remote areas. Encounters with wildlife such as bears are possible, as well as with cattle, horses, and dogs.

There is always the danger of falling and getting swept away when walking in rushing water or on wet, slippery stones. Every year, a few fly fishermen drown. Most anglers wear wader belts or other floatation devices. Some carry a wading staff to test the depth of the water. Fly fishing is an enjoyable sport, but it is vitally important to use caution, carry a first-aid kit, and have an awareness of the surrounding area.

Glossary

ANADROMOUS

Fish that spend much of their lives in saltwater, but swim up freshwater rivers to spawn. Steelhead and striped bass are anadromous.

CATCH AND RELEASE

A practice where anglers catch a fish, sometimes photograph or weigh it, and then release it nearly unharmed back into the water it came from. For threatened or endangered fish, this is an excellent conservation method.

DORSAL FIN

The fin that is located on the top of a fish's back. On a shark, for example, the dorsal fin is the one that sticks out of the water when the shark is swimming near the surface.

DRY FLY

A type of fishing fly that remains on the surface of the water and usually looks like an adult insect. It is made of non-water-absorbent materials.

LEADER

An 8- to 9-foot (2.4- to 2.7-m) section of nylon monofilament or fluorocarbon line between the fly line and the fly. It is tapered and nearly invisible underwater. It is designed to deliver the fly softly, and away from the fly line.

MIMIC

When something looks or acts like something else.

NYMPH

In fly fishing, a fly that mimics the insect stage between the worm-like larva and the adult.

POLARIZED SUNGLASSES

Sunglasses that reduce glare reflected at some angles off shiny non-metallic surfaces such as water. Fly fishermen wear polarized sunglasses to see fish in the water.

STREAMER

A fly that mimics various species of baitfish and other aquatic prey upon which large game fish feed. Usually, feathers or hair are used to create the lures.

TIPPET

The smallest diameter section of a tapered leader. The fly is tied onto the tippet.

WET FLY

In fly fishing, a fly that is weighted enough to drop just below the water's surface. Wet flies look like newborn insects called nymphs.

Index